ICHTHYOSAURS

By Susan H. Gray

THE CHILD'S WORLD®
CHANHASSEN, MINNESOTA

Published in the United States of America by The Child's World®
PO Box 326, Chanhassen, MN 55317-0326
800-599-READ
www.childsworld.com

Content Adviser:
Brian Huber, PhD,
Curator, Department
of Paleobiology,
Smithsonian
National Museum
of Natural History,
Washington D.C.

Photo Credits: Illustration by Karen Carr: 6; Joe McDonald/Corbis: 7; Myron Jay
Dorf/Corbis: 15; Lynda Richardson/Corbis: 23; Bettmann/Corbis: 26; Mike Fredericks:
19; Douglas Henderson: 16, 17; Bob Daemmrich/The Image Works: 25; the Natural
History Museum, London: 5, 8, 13, 14, 18, 24; John Sibbick/the Natural History
Museum, London: 22; Chris Butler/Photo Researchers, Inc.: 4; Biophoto Associates/
Photo Researchers, Inc.: 9; Lawrence Naylor/Photo Researchers, Inc.: 10; Mauro
Fermariello/Photo Researchers, Inc.: 11; Science Photo Library/Photo Researchers,
Inc.: 21; Ben Kear/South Australian Museum: 27.

The Child's World®: Mary Berendes, Publishing Director

Editorial Directions, Inc.: E. Russell Primm, Editorial Director; Pam Rosenberg,
Line Editor; Katie Marsico, Associate Editor; Matthew Messbarger, Editorial Assistant;
Susan Hindman, Copy Editor; Melissa McDaniel, Proofreader; Tim Griffin/IndexServ,
Indexer; Olivia Nellums, Fact Checker; Dawn Friedman, Photo Researcher; Linda
S. Koutris, Photo Selector

Original cover art by Todd Marshall

The Design Lab: Kathleen Petelinsek, design; Kari Thornborough, page production

Library of Congress Cataloging-in-Publication Data
Gray, Susan Heinrichs.
  Ichthyosaurs / by Susan H. Gray.
    p. cm. — (Exploring dinosaurs & prehistoric creatures)
  Includes index.
  ISBN 1-59296-366-8 (lib. bd. : alk. paper) 1. Ichthyosaurus—Juvenile literature. I.
Title.
  QE862.I2G73 2005
  567.9'37—dc22   2004018061

TABLE OF CONTENTS

CHAPTER ONE

4 Dining in the Dark

CHAPTER TWO

7 What Were Ichthyosaurs?

CHAPTER THREE

10 Aren't Ichthyosaurs Just Dolphins?

CHAPTER FOUR

16 Many Different Ichthyosaurs

CHAPTER FIVE

22 What Did Ichthyosaurs Do All Day?

CHAPTER SIX

25 The Hunt for Ichthyosaurs

28 Glossary

28 Did You Know?

29 How to Learn More

30 The Geologic Time Scale

32 Index

DINING IN THE DARK

he ichthyosaur (IK-thee-o-SAWR) took a deep breath and disappeared below the waves. He swam near the surface for a short while and then began to go deeper. As he swam, his tail moved slowly back and forth. With gentle movements of his fins, he steered himself downward.

As the **reptile** descended, he felt the water getting colder. The cold penetrated his body and made it harder to move. It made his muscles stiff and slow. Still, he went deeper.

Ichthyosaurs were amazingly strong swimmers and were able to dive deep in search of food.

*Their swimming and diving skills, powerful jaws, and razor-sharp
teeth helped to make ichthyosaurs fierce hunters.*

As he continued downward, light from the sun slowly faded, and
his surroundings became dark gray. The sounds changed, too, as everything grew quiet. Deeper he went.

The water became almost pitch black, and the ichthyosaur
opened his eyes wide. Although barely a hint of sunlight remained, he
could see everything. He had the biggest eyes of any creature in the
ocean. He saw schools of fish, another ichthyosaur, and, in the dis-
tance, a slow-moving squid. With a sudden burst of speed, he went

Like many modern-day whales, ichthyosaurs preferred a diet of squid.

after the squid. When he was almost upon it, he opened his large

mouth and sucked the squid right in. The ichthyosaur paused a

moment while the animal slipped down his throat. Then he headed

back up to the surface. He desperately needed another breath.

CHAPTER TWO

WHAT WERE ICHTHYOSAURS?

I chthyosaurs were swimming reptiles that lived in the ocean

from about 240 million to 90 million years ago. The word

ichthyosaur is taken from Greek words meaning "fish lizard," because

these animals looked a lot like lizards. However, the ichthyosaurs were

Although much smaller and better suited to life on land, this green iguana is a distant relative of the prehistoric ichthyosaurs.

Unlike dinosaurs, ichthyosaurs died out about 90 million years ago.

neither fish nor lizards. They were a different kind of reptile that lived

at the same time as the dinosaurs. They died out about 25 million years

before the dinosaurs did.

There were many different kinds of ichthyosaurs. All were

streamlined animals with long, narrow jaws, big tails, and fins. The

smallest grew to a length of about 3 feet (1 meter). The largest was 49

feet (15 m) long. Some, but not all, ichthyosaurs had a dorsal (DORE-

suhl) fin. This is a fin that sticks up from the center of the back.

The ichthyosaurs also had two pairs of fins on their sides—a pair in front and a pair in back. In some animals, the fins were all about the same size. In others, the back fins were much smaller than those in front. Ichthyosaurs used their fins mainly for steering and slowing down.

They swam by moving their tails back and forth. Sometimes, such as when chasing **prey,** they flapped their tails quite forcefully. This probably made them look as though they were wiggling through the water.

The hardened remains of ichthyosaur fins help scientists to understand how the reptile moved through prehistoric waters.

CHAPTER THREE

AREN'T ICHTHYOSAURS JUST DOLPHINS?

I f you look at pictures of ichthyosaurs, you will probably think

that they look a lot like dolphins. After all, they both have long

snouts, streamlined bodies, and pairs of fins. What's more, the

ichthyosaurs, like modern-day dolphins, had to

breathe air. So how do we know that

ichthyosaurs weren't just the

dolphins of long ago?

Paleontologists (PAY-lee-

un-TAWL-uh-jists) tell us this

is impossible. Paleontologists

are scientists who study

ancient living things. They

One of the main differences between ichthyosaurs and modern-day dolphins is that ichthyosaurs were reptiles, while dolphins are mammals.

By studying fossil remains, paleontologists are often able to determine what an animal ate, when and where it lived, and possibly even how fast it moved.

look at the **fossils** left behind by plants and animals, and they tell

us how those things lived.

Paleontologists also study the rocks where fossils are found.

They have ways of figuring out just how old those rocks are.

Suppose a paleontologist finds an animal skeleton buried inside

a rock that is known to be 100 million years old. Then the scientist

will know that the animal lived and died 100 million years ago.

Paleontologists have found ichthyosaur bones in rocks that are

90 million years old. But so far, no one has found an ichthyosaur in

younger rocks. People have looked everywhere, but the ichthyosaurs

just aren't there. This tells us that the animals probably died out about

90 million years ago.

The oldest dolphin skeletons ever found were in rocks known

to be about 55 million years old. Although paleontologists have

searched very hard, no one has found dolphin bones in older rocks.

This tells us that the ichthyosaurs and dolphins were two very differ-

ent animals. They never swam together. They never even saw each

other. The ichthyosaurs died out 35 million years before the first

dolphins appeared.

Ichthyosaurs and dolphins are different in other ways, too. The

tail of an ichthyosaur is fishlike. The tail fin spreads out up and down.

Ichthyosaurs used their tail fins to swim like fish.

A dolphin's tail fin spreads out to the sides. As dolphins swim, they paddle their tails up and down. As ichthyosaurs swam, their tails paddled from side to side.

THE BETTER TO SEE YOU WITH

Ichthyosaur skulls show that some of these animals had enormous eyes. *Temnodontosaurus* (TEM-no-DON-toe-SAWR-us) grew to a length of 30 feet (9 m). Its eyes were 10 inches (26 centimeters) across—the size of dinner plates. Another ichthyosaur, *Ophthalmosaurus* (off-THAL-mo-SAWR-us), the "eye lizard," was only 13 feet (4 m) long. Yet its eyes were the size of small Frisbees. A sturdy ring of bone surrounded each eyeball. What can such eyes tell us about these creatures?

To find the answer, we can look at some modern-day animals. Creatures such as owls, cats, and tree-dwelling lorises have large eyes. They also have something else in common. All are nocturnal, or

active at night. Their large eyes help them see objects in the dark.

Inside the eyeball, many animals have two kinds of cells. The cone cells, or cones, help the animals see color. The rod cells, or rods, gather light. Rods and cones form a layer of cells in the back wall of the eye. In animals that move about or hunt at night, this cell layer is loaded with rods. Even in the dark, the rods gather so much light that the animals can see just fine. They may not see colors very well, but that doesn't matter. They just need to see in the dark.

Scientists believe that the ichthyosaurs with the biggest eyes hunted in the darkness of deep-ocean waters. Eyes the size of platters would have had plenty of light-gathering power. Bony rings around the eyes would have supported the eyeballs against the pressure of the ocean's great depths. There probably weren't many prey animals that escaped the notice of those big-eyed, watchful ichthyosaurs.

CHAPTER FOUR

MANY DIFFERENT ICHTHYOSAURS

Ichthyosaurs have been found in Europe, Asia, North America,

South America, and Australia. Scientists tell us there are more than

Cymbospondylus *lived between 248 million and 208 million years ago.*

80 different kinds. The

slender *Cymbospondylus*

(SIM-bo-spon-DEE-

luss) grew to 33 feet

(10 m) in length. It had

small fins on its sides

and no dorsal fin at all.

Its eel-like tail was about

15 feet (4.6 m) long

and came to a point.

Scientists have discovered Shonisaurus *fossils in North America.*

Like other ichthyosaurs, this one had long, narrow jaws built for

catching fish.

Shonisaurus (SHOW-nih-SAWR-us) is the largest ichthyosaur ever

found. *Shonisaurus* measured 49 feet (15 m) from the tip of the snout to the end of the tail. It had an unusually large and rounded belly. Only the very front of the mouth had teeth.

Little *Mixosaurus* (MIX-o-SAWR-us) was 3 feet (1 m) long as an adult. Its name means "mixed lizard," and it surely looked like a mixture of fish and lizard. The tail of *Mixosaurus* ended with a small, poorly developed fin.

Mixosaurus was among the smallest of the ichthyosaurs.

Ichthyosaurus (IK-thee-o-SAWR-us) was a common and wide-ranging ichthyosaur. Its fossils have been found in Europe, Greenland, and North America. *Ichthyosaurus* had unusually large bones in its

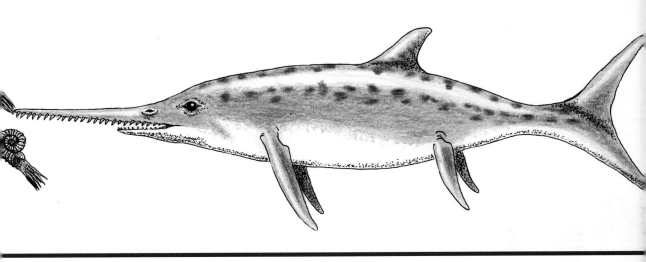

Eurhinosaurus had an unusual beak with teeth that stuck out sideways from its upper jaw. Scientists aren't sure how those unusual teeth were used.

ear. They may have transmitted vibrations from the water, which helped the animal locate prey.

Of all the ichthyosaurs, *Eurhinosaurus* (yoo-RY-no-SAWR-us) had the most unusual beak. Its lower jaw was only half the length of the upper one. Teeth stuck out sideways along both sides of the upper jaw. No one is certain how *Eurhinosaurus* caught its prey or how it used those sideways teeth.

THE FAMOUS FEMALE FOSSILIST

Mary Anning was born in England in 1799. Her family lived in a small town on the seacoast, where her dad made a living as a woodworker. He had another interest as well. Like many people in England at the time, he was fascinated with fossils and ancient life.

When Mary grew old enough, her father began taking her out to look at rocks and fossils. Along the coast, there were some wonderful cliffs where the ocean's waves had worn down the rocks. Mary's dad showed her how to look closely at those rocks and spot the fossils buried inside.

When Mary was only 11, her beloved father died. This left the family in debt and with no one to support them. Mary's dad, however, had given his wife and two children an interest in fossils. So Mary, her brother, Joseph, and her mother got busy.

Joseph and Mary began collecting fossils near their hometown. With their mother's help, they sold them to collectors, schools, and museums. Everyone was amazed at what the children found, and the fossil sales helped the family survive.

One day, Joseph happened to find the skull of an ichthyosaur embedded in rock. It was 12-year-old Mary, however, who excavated the rest of the skeleton. Ichthyosaurs were not well known at the time, and the fossil was seen as a very big scientific discovery.

As the children grew older, Joseph's interest in fossils faded, but Mary's grew stronger. In her early twenties, Mary discovered the first nearly complete skeleton of a *Plesiosaurus* (PLEE-see-o-SAWR-us). This was a kind of swimming reptile with a short, pointed tail and a long neck. She also found an excellent skeleton of a pterosaur (TEHR-us-sawr), one of the great flying reptiles.

Mary kept hunting fossils until she died. By then, museums all over Europe owned fossils that she had found. Mary's discoveries earned her the respect of scientists everywhere. They called her the Princess of Paleontology and "the most famous female fossilist."

CHAPTER FIVE

WHAT DID ICHTHYOSAURS
DO ALL DAY?

chthyosaurs spent much of their time chasing down prey,

eating, and resting. While some probably hunted near the

surface, others dove to great depths. With their long snouts and

sharp teeth, ichthyosaurs were perfectly built for catching and

holding on to prey. Many ichthyosaur skeletons have been found

with the remains of their last meals inside. These fossils show us

Many ichthyosaurs hunted squid (shown here), but scientists believe
that some also used their powerful jaws to catch and eat shellfish.

that the animals ate fish, baby

turtles, and squid.

The ichthyosaurs

with especially huge

eyes were able to

hunt in the dark,

either at night or

deep in the ocean.

It seems that some

These loggerhead turtle hatchlings would have been a tasty meal for an ichthyosaur.

ichthyosaurs dove deeper than they should have. Ichthyosaur

bones show that some of the animals had "the bends." This is a

terribly painful sickness that deep-sea divers sometimes get. When

they dive to great depths and come up too quickly, air moves into

their tissues and forms bubbles. These air bubbles can cause severe

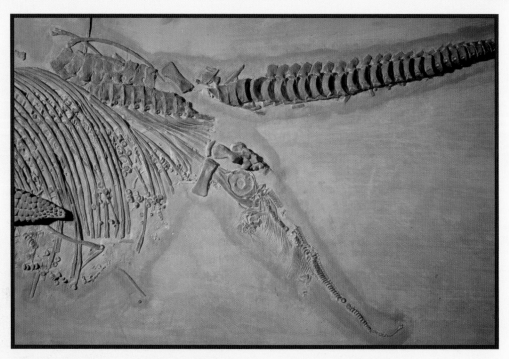

*Fossilized skeletons containing unborn babies show that
ichthyosaurs, like dolphins, gave birth to live young.*

pain in the joints, a loss of feeling, and convulsions. An

ichthyosaur with the bends probably did not survive for long.

At some time during the year, ichthyosaurs did their best to

attract mates. The females did not lay eggs as many other reptiles

do. Instead, they gave birth to live babies. In fact, scientists have

found many adult skeletons with the baby skeletons still inside.

CHAPTER SIX

THE HUNT
FOR ICHTHYOSAURS

You might think that scientists are always the ones who find ichthyosaur fossils. This is not the case. Mary Anning was no scientist when she dug up her famous ichthyosaur. She was about the age of a sixth grader.

In the early 1900s, miners in Nevada found the bones of the giant *Shonisaurus.* Not knowing what they were, the

You don't have to be a scientist to hunt for fossils. Sometimes teachers and their students go on field trips to look for fossils.

*In the early 1900s, Nevada miners had no idea that
they had uncovered the remains of a giant ichthyosaur.*

miners used some of its big, flat backbones for dinner plates. They

made other bones into decorations. In time, word got out about the

discovery, and paleontologists came to excavate.

In the 1970s, some Australians doing roadwork found part of an ichthyosaur skeleton. Scientists came out to hunt for the rest of it but found nothing. Thirty years later, a fence builder was in the same area when he came upon something unusual. He had discovered the rest of the skeleton. Clearly, scientists are not the only people who find ichthyosaurs. In fact, someone reading this book could make the next big discovery.

Sometimes people find only parts of an animal's skeleton, such as this ichthyosaur skull found in Australia.

Glossary

ancient (AYN-shunt) Something that is ancient is very old. Paleontologists study ancient life.

cells (SELZ) Cells are the smallest units that make up living things. Inside the eyeball, many animals have two kinds of cells that help see color and gather light.

excavated (EK-skuh-vate-uhd) Something that is excavated is dug out and removed. Twelve-year-old Mary Anning excavated an ichthyosaur skeleton.

fossils (FOSS-uhlz) Fossils are the things left behind by ancient plants or animals, such as skeletons or footprints. When more fossils are discovered, scientists will learn more about ichthyosaurs.

prey (PRAY) Animals that are hunted and eaten by others are called prey. When chasing prey, ichthyosaurs may have flapped their tails quite forcefully.

reptile (REP-tile) A reptile is an air-breathing animal that has a backbone and is usually covered with scales or plates. Ichthyosaurs were swimming reptiles that lived in the ocean from about 240 million to 90 million years ago.

streamlined (STREEM-lined) If something is streamlined, it is designed so that it moves through air or water quickly and easily. Ichthyosaurs were streamlined animals with long, narrow jaws, big tails, and fins.

Did You Know?

▸ Paleontologists have found fossilized droppings of ichthyosaurs. These are called coprolites (KOP-ro-lites).

▸ Like *Eurhinosaurus*, the modern-day sawfish has a snout lined with many sideways teeth.

▸ *Shonisaurus* is the state fossil of Nevada.

How to Learn More

AT THE LIBRARY

Lambert, David, Darren Naish, and Liz Wyse. *Dinosaur Encyclopedia: From Dinosaurs to the Dawn of Man.*
New York: Dorling Kindersley, 2001.

Palmer, Douglas, Barry Cox (editor). *The Simon & Schuster Encyclopedia of Dinosaurs & Prehistoric Creatures:
A Visual Who's Who of Prehistoric Life.* New York: Simon & Schuster, 1999.

ON THE WEB

Visit our home page for lots of links about ichthyosaurs:
http://www.childsworld.com/links.html
Note to Parents, Teachers, and Librarians: We routinely verify our Web links
to make sure they're safe, active sites—so encourage your readers to check them out!

PLACES TO VISIT OR CONTACT

American Museum of Natural History
*To view numerous fossils and learn more
about prehistoric creatures*
Central Park West at 79th Street
New York, NY 10024-5192
212/769-5100

Carnegie Museum of Natural History
*To view a variety of dinosaur skeletons, as well
as fossils of other extinct animals*
4400 Forbes Avenue
Pittsburgh, PA 15213
412/622-3131

Royal Ontario Museum
*To learn more about the museum's large
collection of ichthyosaur fossils*
100 Queen's Park
Toronto, Ontario
M5S 2C6
416/586-5549

Smithsonian National Museum
of Natural History
*To see several fossil exhibits and take special
behind-the-scenes tours*
10th Street and Constitution Avenue NW
Washington, DC 20560-0166
202/357-2700

The Geologic Time Scale

CAMBRIAN PERIOD

Date: 540 million to 505 million years ago
Most major animal groups appeared by the end of this period. Trilobites were common and algae became more diversified.

ORDOVICIAN PERIOD

Date: 505 million to 440 million years ago
Marine life became more diversified. Crinoids and blastoids appeared, as did corals and primitive fish. The first land plants appeared. The climate changed greatly during this period—it began as warm and moist, but temperatures ultimately dropped. Huge glaciers formed, causing sea levels to fall.

SILURIAN PERIOD

Date: 440 million to 410 million years ago
Glaciers melted, sea levels rose, and Earth's climate became more stable. Plants with vascular systems developed. This means they had parts that helped them conduct food and water.

DEVONIAN PERIOD

Date: 410 million to 360 million years ago
Fish became more diverse, as did land plants. The first trees and forests appeared at this time, and the earliest seed-bearing plants began to grow. The first land-living vertebrates and insects appeared. Fossils also reveal evidence of the first ammonoids and amphibians. The climate was warm and mild.

CARBONIFEROUS PERIOD

Date: 360 million to 286 million years ago
The climate was warm and humid, but cooled toward the end of the period. Coal swamps dotted the landscape, as did a multitude of ferns. The earliest reptiles appeared on Earth. Pelycosaurs such as *Edaphosaurus* evolved toward the end of the Carboniferous period.

PERMIAN PERIOD

Date: 286 million to 248 million years ago
Algae, sponges, and corals were common on the ocean floor. Amphibians and reptiles were also prevalent at this time, as were seed-bearing plants and conifers. However, this period ended with the largest mass extinction on Earth. This may have been caused by volcanic activity or the formation of glaciers and the lowering of sea levels.

TRIASSIC PERIOD

Date: 248 million to 208 million years ago
The climate during this period was warm and dry. The first true mammals appeared, as did frogs, salamanders, and lizards. Evergreen trees made up much of the plant life. The first dinosaurs, including *Coelophysis*, existed on Earth. In the skies, pterosaurs became the earliest winged reptiles to take flight. In the seas, ichthyosaurs and plesiosaurs made their appearance.

JURASSIC PERIOD

Date: 208 million to 144 million years ago
The climate of the Jurassic period was warm and moist. The first birds appeared at this time, and plant life was more diverse and widespread. Although dinosaurs didn't even exist in the beginning of the Triassic period, they ruled Earth by Jurassic times. *Allosaurus, Apatosaurus, Archaeopteryx, Brachiosaurus, Compsognathus, Diplodocus, Ichthyosaurus, Plesiosaurus,* and *Stegosaurus* were just a few of the prehistoric creatures that lived during this period.

CRETACEOUS PERIOD

Date: 144 million to 65 million years ago
The climate of the Cretaceous period was fairly mild. Many modern plants developed, including those with flowers. With flowering plants came a greater diversity of insect life. Birds further developed into two types: flying and flightless. Prehistoric creatures such as *Ankylosaurus, Edmontosaurus, Iguanodon, Maiasaura, Oviraptor, Psittacosaurus, Spinosaurus, Triceratops, Troodon, Tyrannosaurus rex,* and *Velociraptor* all existed during this period. At the end of the Cretaceous period came a great mass extinction that wiped out the dinosaurs, along with many other groups of animals.

TERTIARY PERIOD

Date: 65 million to 1.8 million years ago
Mammals were extremely diversified at this time, and modern-day creatures such as horses, dogs, cats, bears, and whales developed.

QUATERNARY PERIOD

Date: 1.8 million years ago to today
Temperatures continued to drop during this period. Several periods of glacial development led to what is known today as the Ice Age. Prehistoric creatures such as glyptodonts, mammoths, mastodons, *Megatherium,* and saber-toothed cats roamed Earth. A mass extinction of these animals occurred approximately 10,000 years ago. The first human beings evolved during the Quaternary period.

Index

Anning, Joseph, 20, 21
Anning, Mary, 20, 21, *21*, 25

babies, 24, *24*
"bends," 23–24
breathing, 6, 10

cone cells, 15
Cymbospondylus, 16, *16*

dolphins, 10, *10*, 12, 13
dorsal fins, 8

ears, 18
Eurhinosaurus, 19
eyes, 5, 14–15, 23

fins, 8–9, *9*, 12–13, *13*, 16, 18
food, 6, *6*, 9, 15, 16, 22–23, *22*
fossils, 11, *11*, 18, 20–21, 22–23, *24*, 25, *25*,
    27

ichthyosaurs, *4, 5, 6, 9, 13, 14, 16, 17, 18,
    22, 24, 27*
Ichthyosaurus, 18
iguanas, *7*

jaws, 8, 16, 19

miners, 26, *26*
Mixosaurus, 18, *18*

name, 7

Opthalmosaurus, 14
owls, 14, *15*

paleontologists, 10–12, *11*, 26
Plesiosaurus, 21
pterosaurs, 21

rod cells, 15

Shonisaurus, 17, *17*, 26
sizes, 16, 17, 18
squid, 5–6, *6, 22*, 23
swimming, 4–5, 9

tails, 8, 9, 12–13, *13*
teeth, 17, 19, 22
Temnodontosaurus, 14
turtles, 23, *23*

About the Author

Susan H. Gray has bachelor's and master's degrees in zoology
and has taught college-level courses in biology. She first fell in love
with fossil hunting while studying paleontology in college. In her
25 years as an author, she has written many articles for scientists
and researchers, and many science books for children. Susan enjoys
gardening, traveling, and playing the piano. She and her husband,
Michael, live in Cabot, Arkansas.